T0042174

## Life Around the World

# Clothes in Many Cultures

Revised Edition

by Heather Adamson

Consulting Editor: Gail Saunders-Smith, PhD

CAPSTONE PRESS
a capstone imprint

Pebble Plus is published by Capstone Press,
1710 Roe Crest Drive, North Mankato, Minnesota 56003.
www.mycapstone.com

Copyright © 2008, 2016 by Capstone Press, a Capstone imprint. All rights reserved.
No part of this publication may be reproduced in whole or in part, or stored in a retrieval system, or transmitted in any form or by any means, electronic, mechanical, photocopying, recording, or otherwise, without written permission of the publisher. For information regarding permission, write to Capstone Press,
1710 Roe Crest Drive, North Mankato, Minnesota 56003.

**Library of Congress Cataloging-in-Publication Data is available on the Library of Congress website.**
ISBN: 978-1-5157-4288-3 (hardback)
ISBN: 978-1-5157-4237-1 (paperback)
ISBN: 978-1-5157-4357-6 (ebook pdf)

**Editorial Credits**
Sarah L. Schuette, editor; Alison Thiele, set designer; Kara Birr, photo researcher

**Photo Credits**
Capstone Press: Design Element (map); Getty Images: Michael Sewell, 7; iStockphoto: andresr, 5; Shutterstock: Dario Diament, 1, Elena Elisseeva, 20, Geir Olav Lyngfjell, 9, Inna Tyshchenko, 15, J.T. Lewis, 19, leungchopan, 11, Lincoln Rogers, 17, Suriya99, Cover; Thinkstock: Anne Greenwood, 13

## Note to Parents and Teachers

The Life around the World set supports national social studies standards related to culture and geography. This book describes and illustrates clothes in many cultures. The images support early readers in understanding the text. The repetition of words and phrases helps early readers learn new words. This book also introduces early readers to subject-specific vocabulary words, which are defined in the Glossary section. Early readers may need assistance to read some words and to use the Table of Contents, Glossary, Read More, Internet Sites, and Index sections of the book.

Printed in the United States 4526

# Table of Contents

Clothes to Wear . . . . . 4
Work Clothes. . . . . 10
Traditional Clothes . . . . . 14
Your Clothes . . . . . 20

Glossary . . . . . 22
Read More . . . . . 23
Internet Sites. . . . . 23
Index . . . . . 24

# Clothes to Wear

Around the world,
everyone wears clothes
for work or play.

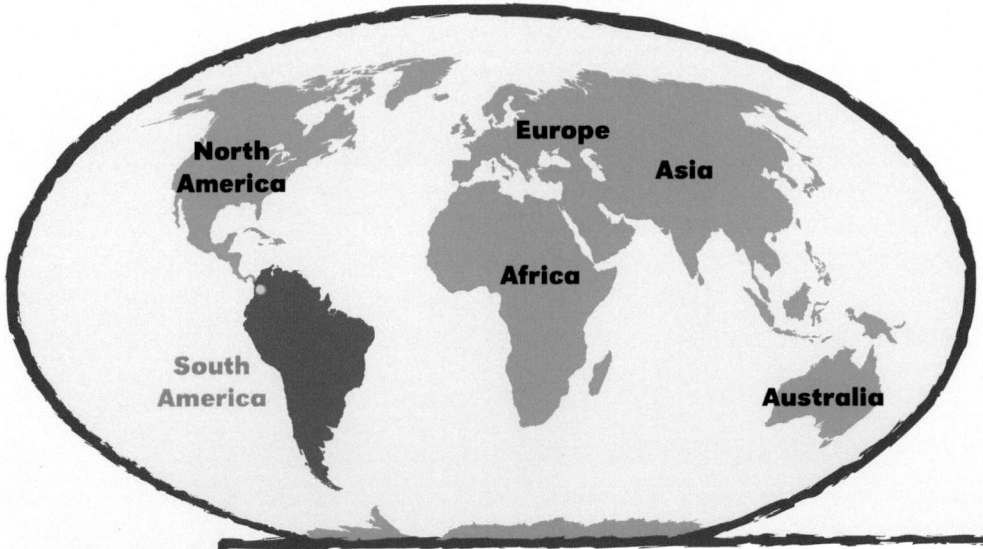


Colombia

Parkas keep people warm
on cold days.

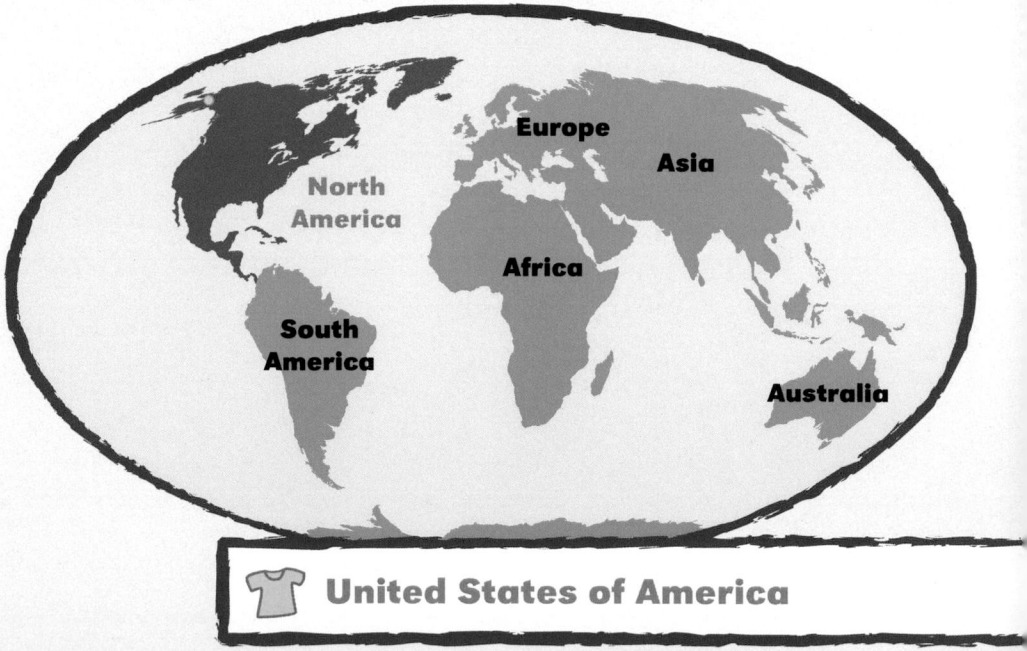

Sarongs keep people cool
on hot days.

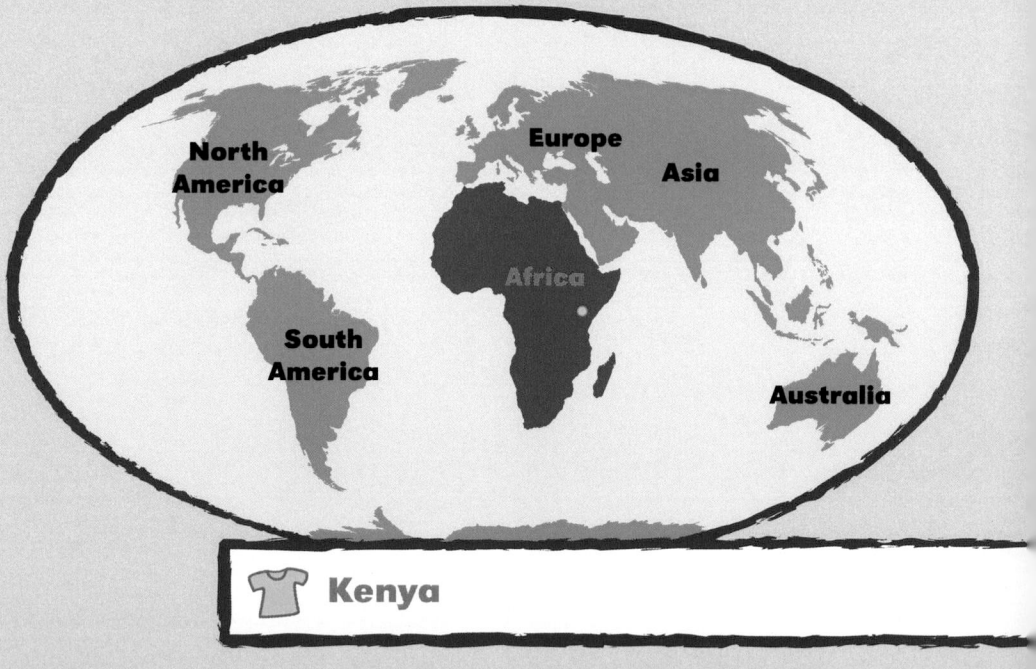

# Work Clothes

Office workers wear business suits to their jobs.

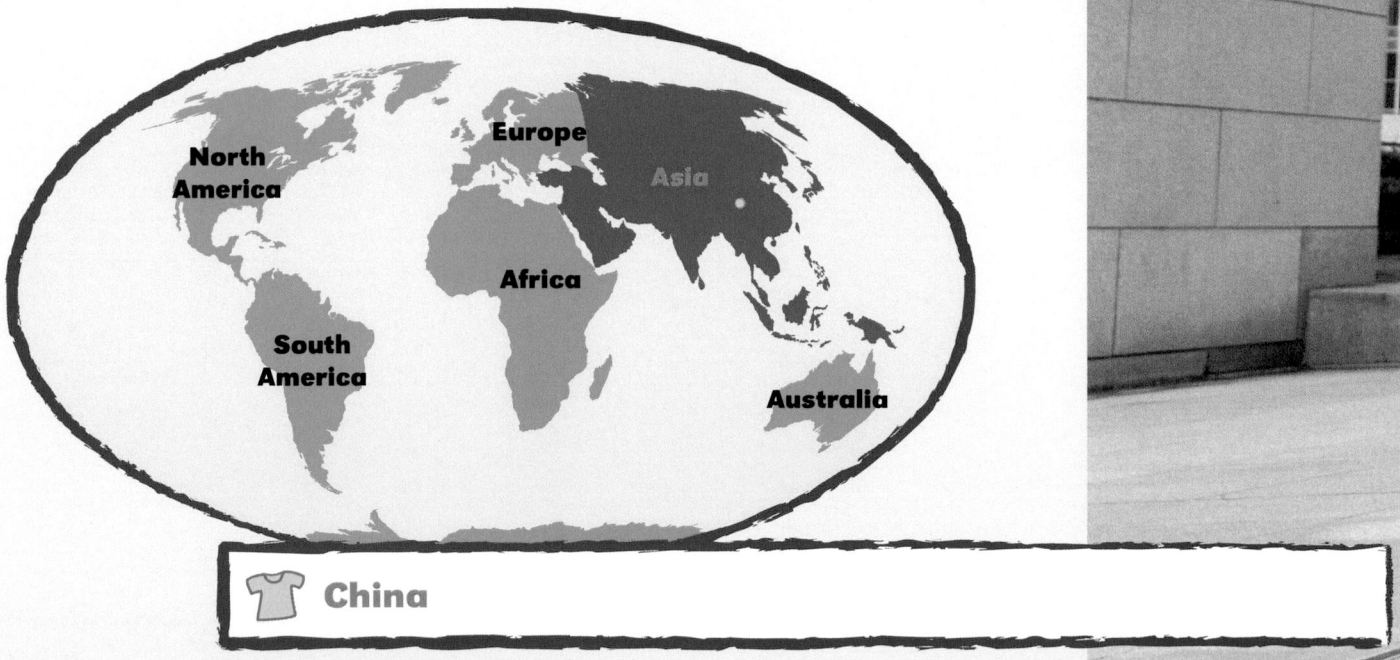

Ranchers wear sturdy jeans when they work outside.

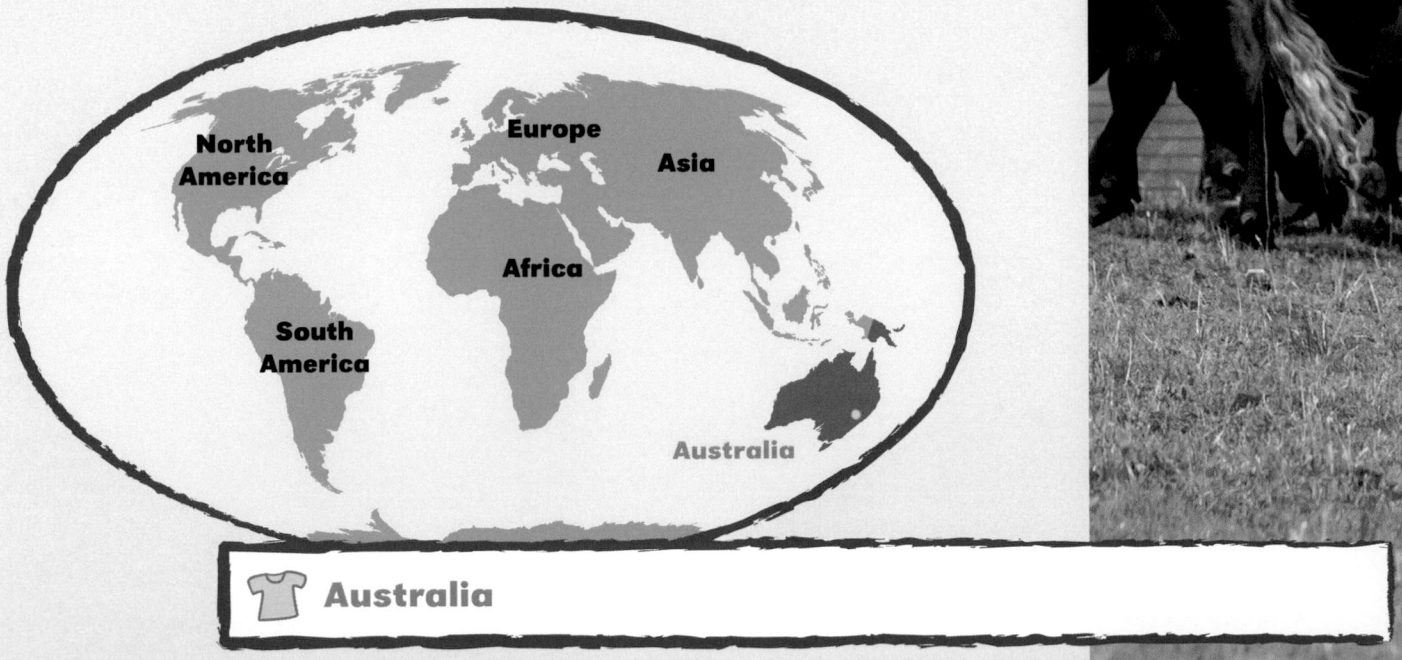

# Traditional Clothes

Brides and grooms wear
fancy clothes
on their wedding day.

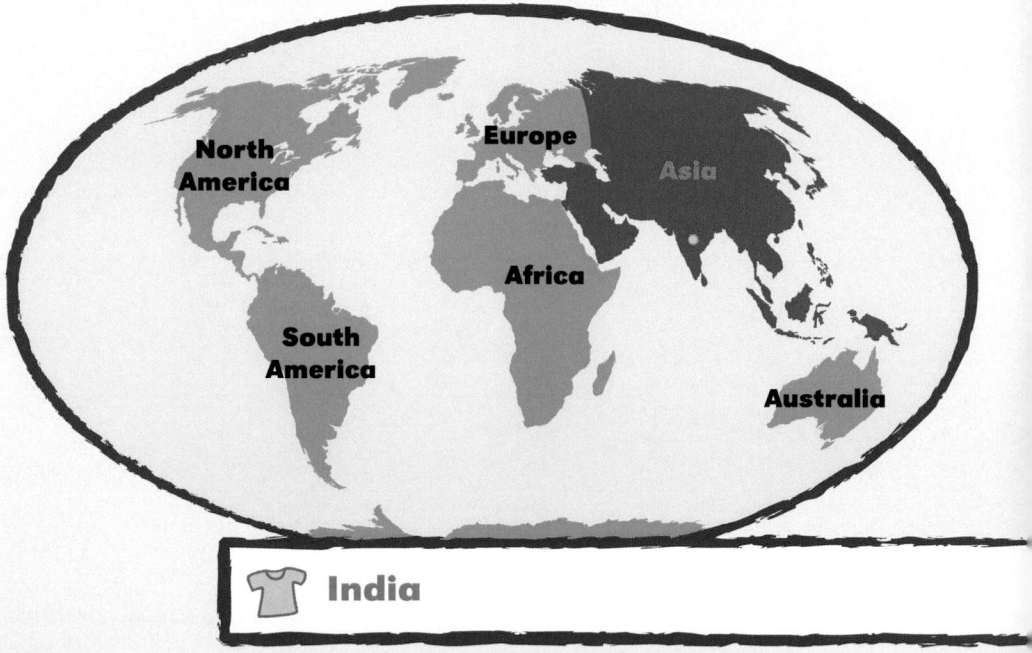

American Indians wear bright colors to dance at powwows.

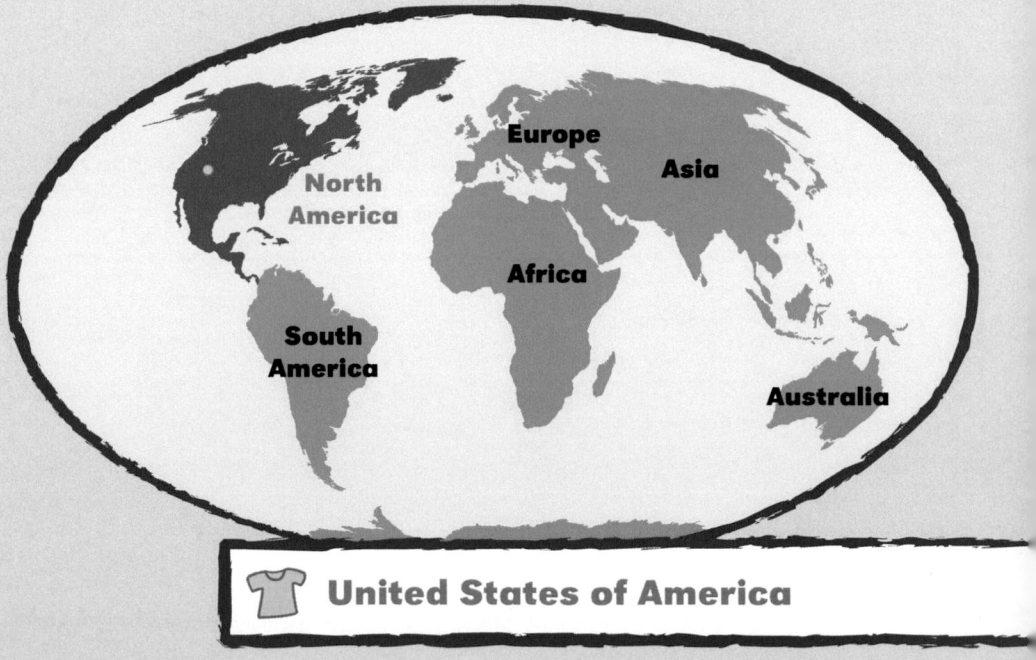

Scottish men wear
kilts in parades
and at ceremonies.

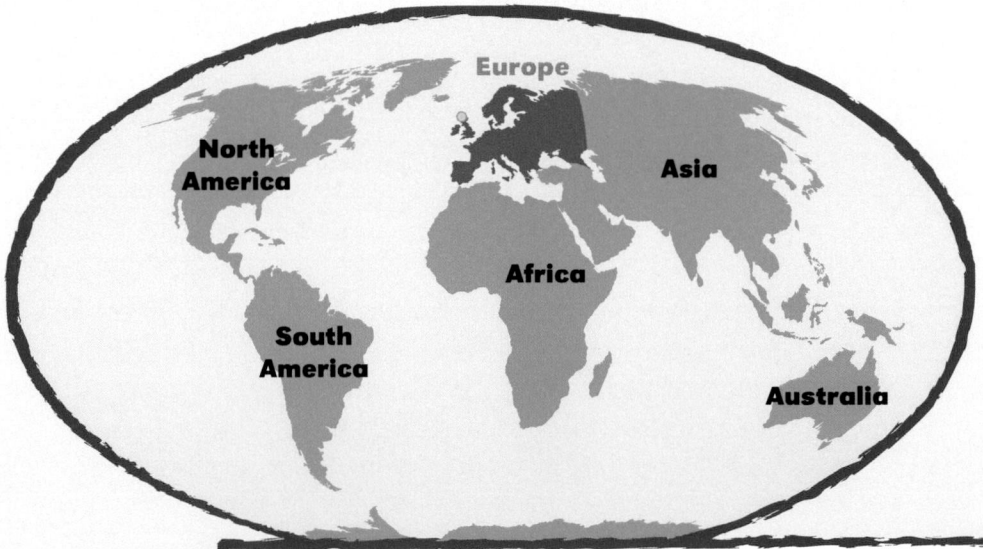


Scotland

# Your Clothes

Clothes are different
around the world.
What did you wear today?

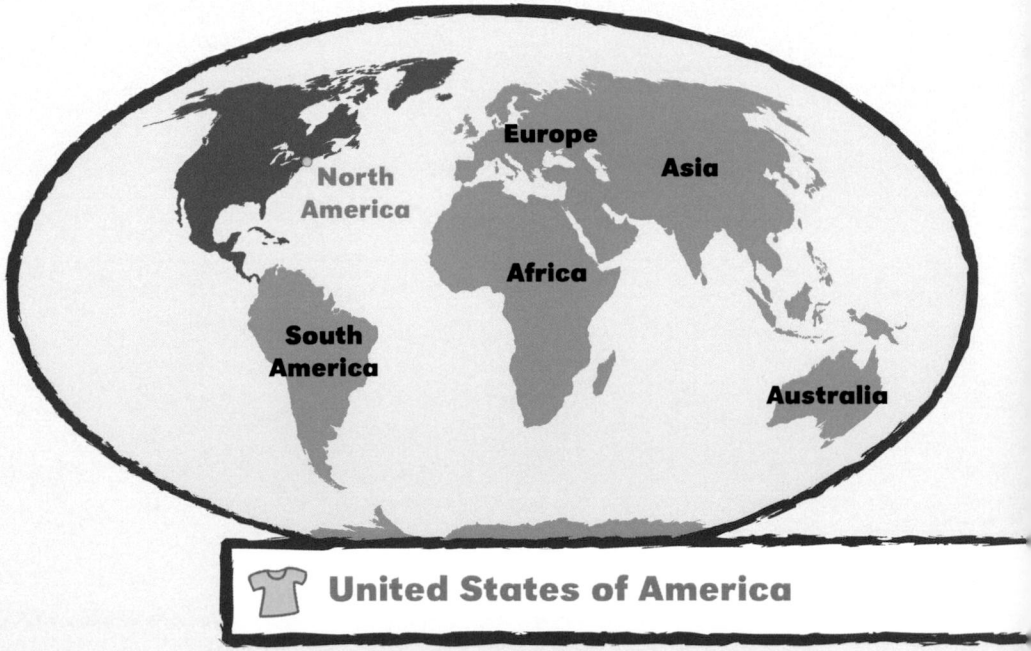

# Glossary

bride—a woman who is about to get married

business suit—a set of matching clothes that includes a jacket and pants or a jacket and skirt

ceremony—formal actions, words, and music performed to mark an important occasion

groom—a man who is about to get married

kilt—a plaid skirt with pleats or folds

parka—a large heavy coat made with fur

powwow—a social gathering where American Indians dance, tell stories, and celebrate traditions

sarong—a piece of cloth wrapped around the body

sturdy—strong and firm; jeans are sturdy and do not rip or tear easily.

# Read More

**Doudna, Kelly.** *Clothing around the World.* Around the World. Edina, Minn.: Abdo, 2004.

**Easterling, Lisa.** *Clothing.* Our Global Community. Chicago: Heinemann, 2007.

**Johansen, Heidi Leigh.** *My Clothes.* Getting to Know My World. New York: PowerKids Press, 2005.

# Internet Sites

FactHound offers a safe, fun way to find Internet sites related to this book. All of the sites on FactHound have been researched by our staff.

Here's how:

1. Visit *www.facthound.com*
2. Choose your grade level.
3. Type in this book ID **1429600187** for age-appropriate sites. You may also browse subjects by clicking on letters, or by clicking on pictures and words.
4. Click on the **Fetch It** button.

**FactHound will fetch the best sites for you!**

# Index

American Indians, 16
brides, 14
business suits, 10
ceremonies, 18
colorful clothes, 16
cool clothes, 8
fancy clothing, 14
grooms, 14
jeans, 12
kilts, 18
office workers, 10
parades, 18
parkas, 6
powwows, 16
ranchers, 12
sarongs, 8
warm clothes, 6
work clothing, 4, 10, 12

Word Count: 79
Grade: 1
Early-Intervention Level: 12